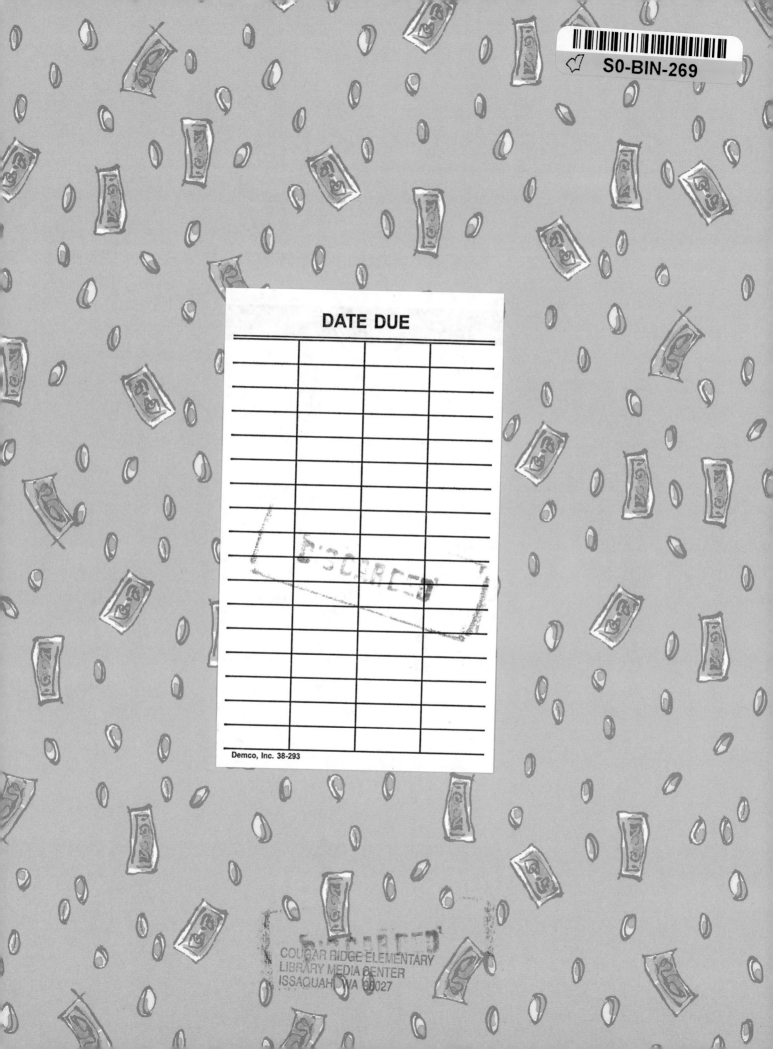

S0-BIN-269

# DATE DUE

| | | | |
|---|---|---|---|
| | | | |
| | | | |
| | | | |
| | | | |
| | | | |
| | | | |
| | | | |
| | | | |
| | | | |
| | | | |
| | | | |
| | | | |
| | | | |
| | | | |
| | | | |
| | | | |
| | | | |

Demco, Inc. 38-293

COUGAR RIDGE ELEMENTARY
LIBRARY MEDIA CENTER
ISSAQUAH WA 98027

# Cowries, Coins, Credit

## The History of Money

First American edition published in 2006 by
Compass Point Books
3109 West 50th Street #115
Minneapolis, MN 55410

Visit Compass Point Books on the Internet at
*www.compasspointbooks.com*
or email your request to
*custserv@compasspointbooks.com*

For Compass Point Books
Catherine Neitge, Brandie E. Shoemaker, Shelly Lyons,
Keith Griffin, and Carol Jones

Copyright © 2006 Allegra Publishing Ltd.
All rights reserved. No part of this book may be reproduced
without written permission from the publisher. The publisher
takes no responsibility for the use of any of the materials or
methods described in this book, nor for the products thereof.
Printed in the United States of America.

For Allegra Publishing Ltd.
Giles Powell-Smith, Will Webster, Mike Phillips
(Beehive Illustration Agency), Rosie Brooks,
Felicia Law, and Karen Foster

Library of Congress Cataloging-in-Publication Data
Bailey, Gerry.
Cowries, coins, credit : the history of money / Gerry Bailey & Felicia
Law.
p. cm. — (My money)
Includes bibliographical references and index.
ISBN 0-7565-1676-5 (hard cover)
1. Money—History—Juvenile literature. I. Law, Felicia. II. Title. III. Series.
HG221.5B25 2006
332.4'9—dc22                    2005030063

The publishers acknowledge the help of Hong Kong Heritage Museum, Hong Kong and
Shanghai Banking Corporation Ltd., and Wong Cheuk Hin for permission to use the
information published on page 37. They also thank Dr. Joseph Santos, associate professor
of economics, South Dakota State University, and Bob Lovitt and Jo Ruff of Greenaway,
Chartered Accountants, Sevenoaks, Kent, UK, for their consultant input.

Photo credits:
© Ann Ronan Picture Library/Heritage Images: 8, 12
© London, British Museum: 8, 9, 10, 11, 12, 30
© The British Library/Heritage Images: 34, 35

# Cowries, Coins, Credit

by Gerry Bailey & Felicia Law

Money has been around in one form or another for 6,000 years—but perhaps not for much longer.

COMPASS POINT BOOKS ✺ MINNEAPOLIS, MINNESOTA

Coin collecting is one of the most popular hobbies in the world!

# Table of Contents

Landmarks in money 6

Barter 8

First coins 9

Coins 10

Records and counting 12

Making money 14

Coin collections 16

Gold 18

Pirates 21

Mining gold 22

Treasure hunting 26

Bullion 28

Paper money 30

Designing notes 32

Forgery 33

Stamps 34

Checks 36

Plastic money 38

International money 40

Glossary 42

Want to Learn More? 45

Index 46

# Landmarks in money

Money is difficult enough to hang on to without it changing its shape all the time! But that's the nature of money. What we use as money today wouldn't be recognized by the ancient people who first started to use money as a way of paying for things. And we probably wouldn't recognize some of the ancient, odd, and downright puzzling kinds of money that were used in the past.

**9000—6000 B.C.**
Cows probably used as first money

**2500 B.C.**
Writing is invented, responding to the need to keep accounts

**3000–2000 B.C.**
Development of "banking" in Mesopotamia

**2250–2150 B.C.**
Cappadocian rulers guarantee quality of silver ingots, which leads to their acceptance as money

**1500 B.C.**
Cowrie shells are used as currency in China

**1355**
Nicole Oresme, economic thinker, argues quantity of precious metal in circulation determines value of currency

**1282**
First recorded "Trial of the Pyx," testing the purity of silver and gold

**1279**
King Edward I issues halfpenny, farthing, and groat (4 pence); day's wages: a penny

**1275–1292**
Marco Polo discovers use of paper money in China

**1232–1253**
Gold coins issued by several Italian states, including Genoa and Florence

**1401**
Bank of Barcelona founded in Spain

**1498**
Problems of long-distance trade routes require that merchants set up investment companies

**1500–1540**
Huge supplies of gold reach Spain from the New World

**1519–1521**
Hernán Cortés notes Aztecs and Mayas use gold dust in hollow quills and cocoa beans as money

**1999**
European single currency adopted—the euro

**1995**
90 percent of the total dollar amount of U.S. money transactions now done electronically

**1980**
Third World debt crisis becomes critical

**1946**
International Monetary Fund (IMF) begins functioning

**1930**
Great Depression

If someone handed you a piece of paper telling you how pure and valuable a shed load of tobacco was, you wouldn't expect to be able to use it to buy a new bicycle. But sometime and somewhere in the past you could.

Or, how about swapping a couple of cows for a television? Oh, and taking a sheep in change. It

sounds bizarre but animals were currency to some people, and not that long ago either.

Let's explore how money came to be, how it changed over the passage of time, and what might be in store for us in the future. But we'll have to go back 6,000 years to understand how it all started.

**1000–220 B.C.**
Miniature tools are used as money in China

**560 B.C.**
In Lydia, crude coins are invented

**600–300 B.C.**
Round, base metal coins are made in China

**600 – 570 B.C.**
Use of coins spreads to Greece

**560 B.C.**
Lydians produce separate gold and silver coins

**336–323 B.C.**
Alexander the Great fixes ratio of silver to gold as ten to one

**1156**
Earliest known foreign exchange contract—115 Genoese pounds reimbursed by 460 bezants in Constantinople

**910**
Issue of paper money in China

**765**
Silver penny becomes main English coin

**269 B.C.**
Romans mint and circulate issue of silver coins

**54–30 B.C.**
Julius Caesar notes Britons still use swords as currency

**323–30 B.C.**
Egyptian granaries used as banks, with central bank at Alexandria; account transfers made for first time

**1519**
Minting of Joachimsthaler, or thaler, in Bohemia; Anglicized, it becomes a dollar

**1553**
First English joint stock company formed—Russia Company

**1566**
Royal Exchange built in England

**1619**
Tobacco used as currency in Virginia

**1633–1672**
Goldsmiths' safes for gold deposits evolve into banks

**1637**
Wampum is legal tender in Massachusetts

**1659**
Earliest English check issued

**1660**
Goldsmiths' notes become bank notes

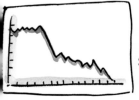

**1929**
Stock market crash

**1913**
U.S. Federal Reserve system founded

**1799**
English Prime Minister Pitt introduces income tax

**1793**
U.S. Mint starts operations

**1782**
Bank of North America is chartered

# Barter

How many times do you swap your possessions with your friends? Or do you insist on a cash payment? Before coins were invented, the only way to trade was to pay for goods you wanted with goods you had. Because most people were living off the land, this usually meant swapping a pig for two chickens and a bunch of hay.

This system of trading with goods is called barter. At first, people bartered goods with the next village or tribe, but as they began to make more and more—both necessities such as pots and cloth, and luxuries such as jewelry and wine—traders traveled further and further to exchange goods.

And as trade grew and increased in volume, and barter became cumbersome, a better way was needed. There were lots of problems with barter—not least the fact that you needed to barter something you didn't need for something you did—and getting the right match wasn't always that easy. So it was only a matter of time before pieces of silver and gold took over as a common exchange. Precious metals, especially gold and silver, were chosen because they were valuable in their own right.

Unlike barter goods, money could act as a standard measure of value, so everyone would know how much an ox or duck was worth in gold coins. Money also helped in keeping accounts, or records of earnings and losses. Money made storing and borrowing wealth easier. Money has worked so well that it's stayed around for thousands of years.

## Cowrie cash

As long ago as 1500 B.C., people in China used a small shell called a cowrie as a kind of money. These small, easy-to-carry shells came from islands in the Indian Ocean and were used in trading by many ancient peoples. In fact, the cowrie shell became so important to the Chinese that they used it as their pictogram, or symbol, for money.

Cowrie shells

Cowrie symbol

Bronze cowrie

Later, the Chinese made bronze and copper cowries that were used as metallic coins. These were among the earliest metal objects used as money.

## Tools as cash

The Chinese used other items as money, as well as cowries. These included tools such as spades, knives, and hoes. The real items were too big to carry around in a purse, so miniature tools were made to take their place. These became known as tool coins. No one knows how long ago the first tool coins were made, but it could be as far back as 1000 B.C. The ancient Greeks sometimes used nails as coins, while the ancient Britons used swords.

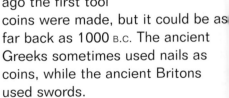

## The Potlatch

A potlatch is a kind of ceremonial feast held by West Coast Native Americans. Sometimes it's held purely for pleasure, but it can also be held to establish new rank or titles among chiefs, or as a kind of trade fair. The trade potlatch was used to boost a chief's status, because wealth was needed to maintain a chief's rank and to distribute wealth among the community. A potlatch might also be held by the members of one village to help another village that had suffered hardship. Sometimes potlatch "wars" broke out when one leader competed for status by giving away more wealth than a rival.

# First coins

The first real coins were made in a country called Lydia around 560 B.C. Lydia was part of what we know today as Turkey. The coins were small lumps of precious metal made of a mixture of gold and silver called electrum. The Lydians stamped each one with the seal of the king to guarantee its value. Later, when the metalworkers became more skilled, they added even more details to the coins. These showed that the coins all had the same weight and metal content and could be trusted to have a standard value when used for trading.

Copy of a gold stater, Iron Age, third century B.C.

Gold stater, Roman, mid-second century B.C.

Electrum stater with a seal, Greek, c. 600–550 B.C.

Gold stater of Hormizd I, Kushanashah, Sasanian empire, c. 276-300

Silver stater with a turtle, Greek, late sixth century B.C.

## Power and prestige

Early coins meant more to their makers than just their value as money. Minting coins gave the city-states of Greece something to boast about. Coins were made as a badge of the city—they weren't just useful but beautiful as well. If a city was able to mint its own coins, everyone knew that it was politically independent.

The Greek city-states were often at war with each other, and this helped to create a more standard system of money, weights, and measures. When one state conquered another, it often forced that state to adopt its currency. Aegina, for instance, was forced to use Athenian "owls" instead of its "turtles" in 456 B.C. Alexander the Great also helped make everything uniform when he conquered the known world. He wanted his coins to show who was top man at the time. Similarly, the Romans used coins to show their subjects who was in charge.

# Greek coins

Once traders saw how useful coins could be, other countries began to make them as well. The use of coins spread to countries like Persia and Greece. The Greeks had first used grain as a kind of currency. Then they turned to nails, or pointed spits. Six nails equaled a handful, or drachma, of grain. One of the smaller Greek coins was called an obol, and by weight six silver obols were worth one silver drachma—the same name as the handful of grain.

Greek coins were round with a picture on both sides, something that still exists today. The design, which might be the seal of a king or ruler, told which city-state had minted, or stamped, the coin. Athenian coins had an owl stamped on them. Some coins had the head of the ruler stamped on one side.

Early Greek coin, front and back

Coins show everyone who's top dog.

- 9 -

# Coins coins coins

From the 1200s, Italian city-states like Venice and Florence issued gold coins. These were called ducats or sequins in Venice and florins in Florence.

The Roman emperors issued gold, silver, and bronze coins. By putting their faces on the coins, they were able to show their people what they looked like and what their titles were.

The first German coins were large silver coins called Joachimsthalers, or thalers. The English translation of thaler is dollar, and this is where the word came from.

The dollar was also adopted in the United States and other countries. In England in 1489, Henry VII issued the first British pound, worth 240 silver pennies. Pound coins are still in use today.

In China, tool coins were replaced by round ones with a square hole in the middle, so they could be threaded on a string.

Similar tool coins were introduced into Japan. In the 1800s, silver dollars were imported into China and Japan. They took over from the traditional forms of money to become yuan in China and yen in Japan.

The bronze sestertius of the Roman emperor Nero, 54–68

The silver denarius of Julius Caesar, 44 B.C.

Silver decadrachm of Syracuse, Greek, c. 413 B.C.

The 4-thaler coin of Christian Ludwig, Duke of Brunswick–Luneburg, 1662

The gold florin was first minted in 1252 in Florence, Italy. Florins were carried from one European country to another by traveling merchants.

Coin of Julius, Duke of Brunswick, Germany, 1576

The gold aureus of Augustus, 27 B.C.– 4 A.D.

Tin pattern for a U.S. silver dollar issued in 1776

Gold pavilion of Edward the Black Prince of Aquitane, 1362

The Greeks forged flat gold discs and decorated them with intricate raised designs.

Silver cistophorus of Augustus, Roman, c. 27 B.C.

Bronze Kaiyuan tongbao coin, China, Tang dynasty, 621

Gold mohur of Jahangir, Agra, India, Mughal dynasty, 1605–1628

19th-century Chinese silver coin with symbol of the imperial dragon

Gold 4-excelentes of Ferdinand V and Isabella, c. 1500

Traditional Shogun coin from Japan

Gold 20 yen coin, Japan Meiji era, 1897

Silver half pagoda of the East India Company, Madras Presidency, south India, 1807

# Records and counting

If you were a trader before writing and mathematics were invented, you'd have to remember every thing you bought or sold, where it was put, and who owed you a sheep or two. You'd also have to trust that the people you dealt with were honest, because there was no record of your transactions. It must have been tough!

Then, in Sumer, a city-state in the ancient country of Mesopotamia (now Iraq), scribes developed the first kind of bookkeeping. They created stone tokens to represent specific kinds of economic items. The tokens were later made of clay. There was a token for sheep, a token for wine, a token for grain, and so on. To record three sheep and two jugs of wine, the Sumerian bookkeeper would make three tokens for sheep and two for wine. These tokens were then stored in a container, probably made of cloth or leather. The quantities and the items were linked together. When the bookkeeper wanted to check his inventory, he looked in the container to see what was inside.

## Pictographs

Around 3000 B.C. the Sumerian scribes developed a more complicated system of counting things. The tokens were replaced by pictographs, or drawings that represented objects, such as a sheep or bird. The pictographs were drawn on a piece of soft clay. Now the quantities and items were separated. The scribe wrote the pictograph for sheep alongside the symbol for the quantity, or number. So, two symbols were used, one for the amount and one for the item. This was a breakthrough.

## Cuneiform writing

At the same time, written symbols developed from pictures into even simpler, more abstract wedge-shaped marks known as cuneiform. And special marks were made to record more abstract words, such as human feelings. So now, cuneiform writing wasn't only used to count or record things, it could be used to tell stories as well.

## Weighing the cash

Today, we count out our money to see how much we've got. But in ancient times people weighed it. A trader would put a handful of coins on a balance to see how much they were worth. People were used to this method. Roman soldiers, for instance, were paid in libres of copper. A libre weighed a pound.

Our words spend, expenditure, and pound all come from the Latin—or Roman—word *expendere*, which means "to weigh."

The drachma was the main unit of weight used by the Greeks, and it's still used as the name of their currency today.

Tablet with cuneiform writing on clay

10    12    Barley

Wool    Bronze

This tablet is one of the earliest on record. It describes the transfer of 300 acres (120 hectares) of land between two parties, using pictographs.

# Adding it up!

## Egypt

Unlike the Mesopotamians, the Egyptians used papyrus to write on. They made lists on papyrus to record all the goods stored in their large granaries. They never got beyond list making, but the accounts had to be accurate. If the authorities found any irregularities, the culprit could be labeled a thief and lose a hand—or even his life!

## Rome

The Romans had the advantage of using coins as currency. This made record keeping a bit easier. The system they used was based on the system used by every Roman citizen. An *adversaria*, or daybook, was filled in to record the daily receipts and payments of each household. Monthly entries were made in a cashbook known as a *codex accepti et expensi*—you can probably figure out what that means without a translation. Keeping records was important in Rome because citizens had to submit regular statements of assets and liabilities, which were used to calculate how much tax they owed. Government accounts were managed by *quaestors*, who had to account for what was in their treasury when they retired.

## England

William the Conqueror became king of England in 1066. Twenty years later, he commissioned the *Domesday Book*, a survey of all the lands owned and taxes due on them in the country. Figures from it were used to create the oldest surviving account record of what a king was owed. It was called the Pipe Roll or Great Roll of the Exchequer. It noted rents, fines, and taxes due to the king from 1130 to 1830.

## Italy

Our modern bookkeeping and accounting procedures date back to Italy in the 1300s. It was then that people began to keep debit and credit records, or a system close to the double entry system. Business was beginning to boom after the so-called Dark Ages. Then in 1494, an Italian mathematician, scholar, and philosopher called Fra Luca Pacioli wrote the first text describing the system. He did it with such clarity and accuracy that it became the standard system for keeping accounts, and still is today.

# Adding Tools

## The Tally Stick

The tally stick was first used in England in the 1300s as a tax record. The sheriff of an area had to collect the taxes and send them to the king. First, though, the tax amount was recorded by cutting notches into a wooden twig. The twig was then split down the middle, and one piece was kept by the sheriff and one by the king. When the tax was due, the sheriff would arrive with the money and his half of the tally stick, which had to fit perfectly with the king's.

## The Quipu

A quipu was a set of different-colored cords with knots made in them attached to a main cord. The Incas of Peru used the quipu for counting and for noting other information. The number of knots, their position, and the colors of the cords all gave specific information. The knots were thought to represent units of 10 and multiples of 10 according to where they were placed. The cord's color probably represented the item that was being counted.

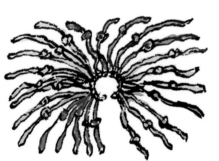

## Abacus

An abacus is a device used for counting and doing mathematical calculations. It was invented thousands of years ago, probably in the Middle East, and is still in use today in some countries. Multiplication is done by repeated addition, while division is done by repeated subtraction. Most abacuses are made up of rows of wire on which rows of beads can be moved from side to side. A skilled abacus user can do calculations almost as fast as a computer can.

# Making money

By the 1500s, coins were in use in almost every country of the world. But they were still weighed and not counted, as they are today. In other words, a coin was worth as much as it weighed and not the value stamped on it, its denomination. People didn't trust that the value stamped on coins was genuine, so the rulers in each country had to guarantee this.

## Royal mints

The monarchs and their governments quickly saw how to turn this to their own benefit. They would get into the business of coin making themselves. In many countries they set up minting factories known as Royal Mints. They guaranteed the authenticity of each coin and allowed an image of their head to be stamped on it. And because the coins were usually worth more than the metal they were made of, the monarchs pocketed the difference!

To increase their profits, the monarchs recalled the coins every few years and issued new ones. In fact, monarchs controlled the mints and the making of coins until the rise of banks and the popular use of paper money.

Kings and queens had total control over money.

There were a number of ways to test the authenticity of a coin. One test was to rub a coin on the surface of a piece of schist or quartz, called a touchstone. The color of the trace of metal left on the stone determined its purity. A second was called the Trial of the Pyx, held in public in front of a jury. The trial involved using 24 touch needles, one for each gold carat. The same method was used for silver.

## Parts of a coin...

### Here are the main parts of a coin:

**relief:** The relief is part of a coin's design that is raised above the surface.

**obverse:** The obverse is the front side, or "heads," of a coin. Generally, it's the side with the date and main design.

**edge:** The edge is the outer border of a coin and is sometimes considered the third side. Edges can be plain, reeded, lettered, or decorated.

**mint mark:** A small letter or symbol on a coin used to identify where it was made. Current U.S. mint marks for coins in circulation are P (Philadelphia) and D (Denver).

**legend:** The legend is the principal inscription, or lettering, on a coin.

**field:** The field is the flat portion of a coin's surface not used for design or inscription.

**rim:** The rim is the raised edge on both sides of a coin (created by the upsetting mill) that helps protect the coin's design from wear.

**reverse:** The reverse is the back side, or "tails," of a coin.

## A Tale of Milling

A milled coin is one that is pressed by a machine rather than hammered.

The first screw press ever used was in England. It was powered by a horse and supervised by a Frenchman called Eloye Mestrelle. Because of his nationality, the British mint workers resented Mestrelle, and after 10 years he was dismissed. He turned to counterfeiting and was hanged for it in 1578. It was 60 years before the mint started milling coins again. Milling produced coins of much better quality and took over from hammering during the next 100 years.

# The process of minting

Every coin we use comes from a currency-making "factory" called a mint. Each country has its own mint and mints, or makes, its own coins. This is how a mint makes its coins:

## 1. Blanking

All coins begin as a metal strip about 13 inches (33 centimeters) wide and 1,500 feet (457 meters) long. The strips are wound into coils, which makes them easier to move around. Each strip is fed into a blanking press that punches out round discs of metal called blanks. What's left, called webbing, is shredded and used again. The U.S. Mint doesn't make blanks for cents. These are brought in after the makers are supplied with copper and zinc by the mint itself.

## 2. Annealing, Washing, and Drying

Because each type of coin is a different size, the blanks are sized accordingly. They're also made up of different combinations of metals. However, they have to be prepared before being minted. First, the blanks are heated and softened in an annealing furnace. Then they pass through a washer and dryer. This preparation makes them very shiny.

## 3. Upsetting

Each coin must have a raised rim, called an upset, around its edge. The rim is milled into the blank as it runs through an upsetting machine. The blank is now a planchet.

## 4. Striking

The next stage is to add the design and lettering to the planchet that will make it a particular coin. This process is called striking. The upset planchets are passed through a press called a coining press that strikes, or presses, the amount, words, and pictures onto them. The planchet has now become a real coin.

## 5. Inspection

Before they can leave the mint, coins have to be inspected. Those that are flawed have to be remade. The press operator uses a magnifying glass to spot-check each new batch. He or she has to make sure the designs and inscriptions come out as they should. After that, the coins go through a coin sizer that screens out any dented or misshapen coins.

## 6. Counting and Bagging

When the coins are ready to be shipped out of the mint, an automatic counting machine drops an amount of coins into a canvas bag.

## 7. Storing coins

Not all minted coins are needed right away. The bags of new coins are loaded onto a pallet and taken by forklift to the storage vault. Storage vaults are rooms inside the mint. Usually they're as well protected as any fortress. Like the rest of the mint, they must be able to withstand fire, earthquake, and of course, robbery. The walls of a storage vault can be up to 2 feet (60 cm) thick.

When new coins are needed they are shipped to a central bank, such as the Federal Reserve or the Bank of England, by armored trucks. From there they are taken to local banks.

## Da Vinci's Coin Minting Invention

One of Leonardo da Vinci's less well-known inventions was a gadget for minting coins quickly. In fact, it was a kind of hammer that could be used for forging a design into precious metals such as gold or silver. At each blow of the hammer, the coin was moved along automatically so that the next piece could be minted. It worked as a kind of money-making assembly line! Da Vinci's drawing of the device, which was done around 1495, was found in one of his drawing books called the *Codex Atlanticus*, which is kept at the Ambrosiana Library in Milan, Italy.

# Coin collections

Coin collecting is one of the most popular hobbies in the world. It can tell you a great deal about the history of the kings, queens, emperors, presidents, and governments that issued the coins and the period in which they lived. It can also tell you about the traders and other people who used them. Many coins are also works of art created by coin designers and can make a spectacular exhibit.

## Who collects coins?

Anyone can collect coins. A collection doesn't have to be made up of expensive examples. All coins can tell some kind of story, even though some are more interesting than others. Many people collect by theme. This means coins may feature kings, boats, animals, or be special-issue coins. Although gold and silver coins cost a lot, most coins are easy to buy and are not expensive. So what are you waiting for? Start collecting now!

### You'll need

- A metal point or toothpick for removing dirt
- A soft toothbrush for cleaning
- A magnifying glass for looking at details
- Rubbing alcohol
- Cotton balls
- A coin tray or some other storage item

## Cleaning

Usually you'll need to clean the coins you collect. Many will have been used over and over again, and some may even have been buried in the ground. You can clean them by using rubbing alcohol and a cotton ball. Dip the cotton in the alcohol and rub gently. Hard-to-remove pieces of dirt can be attacked with a soft toothbrush, a toothpick, or a metal point (as long as it's used carefully). Don't use metal polish or a wire brush because these can damage the coins.

Coins that have been in circulation will need a good cleaning.

## Storing

Most collectors like to store their collection in coin trays. Mahogany wood trays are best for gold or silver coins. Other kinds of wood cause corrosion. Plastic trays can also be used. Don't store coins in plastic envelopes because these can get tacky and also cause corrosion. Paper envelopes work well. They don't cause damage, and you can write on them.

## Recording

Recording your collection is a good way of noting what you've got. You can make a catalog using a notebook. An additional way of noting the coins is to make a coin rubbing, using a pencil lead. Put the paper on top of the coin and rub with the lead. The image of the coin will appear on the paper. You could use rubbing wax rather than a pencil to do a really good job.

# Coin detecting

o begin the fascinating hobby of coin detecting you will need a coin or metal detector. Coin detectors work by creating an electromagnetic field that penetrates the ground to a certain level. When the detector is passed over a metal object, the object causes a change in the field that the detector senses. This sends a signal to the control box and on to a meter or headphones, where it creates a noise.

You need patience to hunt coins. Don't rush over the area you want to cover, but sweep the detector slowly over the ground, keeping it flat. Look for signs of pottery or coal because they might indicate past activity. Remove all the trash items you unearth since you don't want to dig them up again. And fill in any holes you have dug.

If you find something special, make a grid square to keep track of where you found it. Use your footprints to tell where you have been in the grid. Good luck!

# Great coin collections

People have been assembling and enjoying coin collections for hundreds of years. We know, for instance, that the great Italian banking family of the Renaissance, the Medici of Florence, held a wonderful collection. So did another great Italian family, the Este of Milan. These were wealthy families, but people who weren't so rich have also had some great collections. Many of these were sold to museums through the years, so they're available for all to see.

Another great collection is the T. Harrison Garrett collection. Garrett collected gold, silver, copper, and nickel pattern coins. He began in the 1860s and the coins were added to by three further generations.

The Louis Eliasberg collection contains examples of every coin in the *Red Book Guide to U.S. Coins*.

Many museums have coin collections, so it's worth checking them out to see what they've got.

The John Jay Pittman collection is considered to be one of the world's best. Amazingly it was assembled on a tight budget. Pittman collected classic U.S. and world coins, spending about $100,000. At one point he mortgaged his house so he could travel to Egypt to attend the palace sale of King Farouk's collection. However, when Pittman's coins were sold at a series of auctions between 1997 and 1999, they made $30 million.

# Precious gold

Gold is a precious metal. Its chemical sign is Au, which stands for *Aurum*, a Latin word that means "shining dawn." Gold is valued for its softness and its ductility, which means it can be drawn easily into fine wires without breaking. It's also very heavy. It weighs 19 times as much as an equal volume of water. And it conducts electricity easily. When most metals are heated they start to soften. But gold doesn't absorb heat easily, and therefore it holds its shape even when it's very hot. Gold also reflects dangerous infrared light better than any other metal. For this reason it's used to tip the nose on a spacecraft. It's valuable and it's incredibly useful!

Gold has been found in almost every country of the world. Fine veins of this precious metal run through hard rock, and nuggets, or rough chunks, are also discovered in sandy rock.

Sometimes heavy rainstorms wash tiny grains of gold out of the rock and into mountain streams. Today, most of the world's gold comes from the Rand mines in South Africa and from mines in Australia and in the state of Nevada. Deep down inside the mines, in the reefs, or gold-bearing rocks, miners blast away at the rock face with dynamite. Heavy crushers called stamps pound the rock into fine gravel. In every ton of gravel, just 25 tiny grams of gold will be found. And it's expensive. If you had the same weight in gold as the weight of a small bag of potato chips, you'd pay about $500 for it!

Gold is one of the heaviest metals

People were buried with a piece of gold to be used in the next life.

## Gold beliefs

Gold is valued and respected all over the world.

Ghana, a country on the west coast of Africa, was once called the Gold Coast because of its gold supplies. Even today, many people in Ghana believe in the power of gold and think that it will protect them from evil spirits. That's why when a man dies, he is buried holding a piece of gold to take with him to the next life.

In India, the people admire gold for its purity, power, and glory. When a father sees his newborn child, he touches the baby with gold to bring luck. The relatives of a dying person put a speck of gold in the mouth as protection.

In Bengal in the north of India, brides celebrate their wedding day by decorating themselves with gold jewelry. Their saris are woven with gold thread, and they even dab gold dust on their faces. Wearing gold is not only beautiful, it's a sign of prosperity and good luck.

# The legend of El Dorado

The treasure of El Dorado is said to lie at the bottom of a deep lake somewhere in the jungles of South America.

The Spanish were among the first explorers to search for this treasure.

I've heard stories about an Indian tribe that performs an amazing sacrifice whenever a new chief is chosen.

The chief's body is rubbed over with gum, onto which fine gold is then blown.

El Dorado, which means "the golden man" in Spanish, is then carried to the lake.

A long procession of men and women carry precious gifts of gold.

The chief plunges into the lake and the gold dust is washed away.

Because the ceremony is repeated many times, the lake is said to hold a treasure trove.

hurray hurray hurray

With great cheers, the crowd hurls their valuable gifts into the lake.

Many different lakes in South America have been explored by divers, and some have even been drained, but little of the lost treasure has ever been found.

# Spanish gold

Not all the gold that left the Americas for Spain in those fine galleons had been mined from the rock. Much of it was stolen!

In 1532, the Spanish explorer Francisco Pizarro set sail for Peru in South America. He had heard tales of the Inca peoples who lived there and of their incredible hoards of gold and silver. It was said that Inca temples blazed with precious ornaments and statues and that the walls of the emperor's palace were lined with gold.

Pizarro soon found that the stories were true. The mountains of Peru were rich with gold, and the Incas mined and forged it in great quantities.

Pizarro murdered the guards who protected the powerful Inca emperor Atahualpa, and took him prisoner. As a ransom for Atahualpa's release, he demanded that a huge room be stacked with gold. The ornate and richly decorated treasure was then melted down into gold bars and sent back to Spain by ship.

Atahualpa's loyal subjects were forced to obey Pizarro's commands with this huge ransom, only to find that Pizarro was not going to keep his promise. Their king was condemned to die after all.

Other Spanish explorers followed Pizarro. They captured more and more hoards of Inca gold from Peru and Aztec gold from Mexico. They melted it all down into gold bars and shipped it across the sea to Spain in their galleons.

Elsewhere, trading ships were crossing different oceans, laden with valuable goods. These were owned by merchants who traded timber for jewels, silks for perfumes, and carpets for silver coins. Each ship was a floating temptation. They offered quick rewards for the world's pirates, who plundered and robbed any vessel that came in sight.

Goods stolen from treasure ships were known as booty. The captain of a pirate ship would reward his pirate crew with a share of the booty in return for hard work and brave fighting. Of course, the captain always kept the largest share for himself!

## Pieces of eight

Daring pirates were called buccaneers. As soon as the Spanish discovered the treasure mines of Central and South America, they built workshops known as mints. Here they melted down the raw silver and gold and shaped it into large bars. They molded some into gold and silver coins. The largest silver coin was called an Eight Reale piece and was stamped with a figure 8. All the coins became known as pieces of eight. Many modern coins are descended from the original Eight Reale piece.

# Pirates

The greatest pirates were wealthy and powerful.

When Christopher Columbus landed in America in 1492, he proudly claimed it as the property of Spain.

More Spanish ships followed, sailing for both North and South America. They put to port all along the east coast, which became known as the Spanish Main.

The Spanish discovered a vast land rich in timber and minerals. They also found great quantities of gold, silver, and precious stones in the mines of Mexico and Peru.

The Spanish loaded their galleons with treasure and sailed for home.

Pirates from other European countries gathered in Jamaica in the West Indies. They were jealous of Spain's new wealth, so they attacked and plundered the ships returning to Spain laden with treasure.

**Henry Morgan** was a notorious pirate. He buried some of his stolen treasure on an island called Old Providence. Legend says that 50 years later, a sailor called Edward Seward was shipwrecked with his wife on this island. Imagine their surprise and delight when they found a treasure trove stacked with gold coins, crucifixes, jewel-studded swords, and gold chains.

**Cheng I** was a small, hunchbacked Chinese man. He sailed on short pirate raids around the coast of China. He became very rich and his fleet of stolen boats grew until he owned 500 of them. When Cheng I was killed in a typhoon, his wife, Cheng I Sao, took charge of the fleet. She was even fiercer than her husband. Once she defeated 100 ships belonging to the emperor of China. She rewarded her pirates with silver for each victim's head they brought her.

**Barbarossa** led the Barbary Corsairs, a fierce band of pirates who raided trading ships sailing in the Mediterranean, off the coast of Northern Africa. Barbarossa had seen his brother and his army of Corsairs hunted down and killed by the Spanish. He hated them and all the countries that supported them. He took revenge for his brother's death by raiding the coastal villages of France, Italy, and Spain. His pirates carried off the loot, as well as prisoners to be sold as slaves.

**Edward Teach** was another ferocious buccaneer. He had a long, black beard that was twisted into braids with ribbons and which hung down his chest like rats' tails. To frighten his enemies, he put burning matches under his hat and firecrackers in his beard. His nickname was Blackbeard. He sailed for Jamaica to begin his life as a buccaneer. During his life, Blackbeard had 14 wives! He raided ships along the coast of America and lived in great luxury. His crew were well-rewarded with shares of booty—especially rum.

# Mining gold

For as long as people have known there's gold in the ground, there's been a rush to get it out.

## The rush for gold

The Egyptians began mining gold in Egypt, Sudan, and the Arabian Peninsula around 2000 B.C. But by modern standards they didn't mine very much—about 1 ton a year.

- The Romans mined about 5 to 10 tons (4.5 to 9 metric tons), mainly from Spain, Portugal, and Africa.
- During the Middle Ages, gold production—especially in Europe—slowed down, although gold was being mined in South America by the native people.
- By the mid-15th century, Ghana in western Africa, also called the Gold Coast, provided 5 to 8 tons (4.5 to 7 metric tons) a year for Spanish and other adventurers. At the same time, the Spanish and Portuguese conquests in the Americas provided gold from Mexico, Peru, and, later, Brazil.
- Gold also came in high quantities from Russia. But it was the find at Sutter's Mill in California in 1848 that was the turning point in gold mining history. Gold was mined at an amazing rate by previous standards—about 77 tons (69 metric tons) were mined in 1851 alone.
- Gold was then discovered in Australia and South Africa, creating more gold rushes.
- In the last 6,000 years, historians think just over 125,000 tons (112,500 metric tons) of gold have been mined, with 90 percent of it since 1848.

# Wimmer's Nugget

On a cold January morning in 1848, James W. Marshall, a carpenter who was building a sawmill on the American River in California, stuck his hand into a mill wheel and pulled out a shiny metal pellet the size of a split pea.

This looks like gold to me. Hey—we could have a gold mine here.

We've heard about gold bonanzas ...

... that never panned out. It'll be fool's gold, mark my words.

Marshall asked one of his workers, Peter Wimmer, to show the nugget to his wife. Jenny Wimmer had seen gold back in Georgia when she was panning there.

Jenny was the only female in the camp. She'd suggested all along that the shiny specks she'd seen along the riverbank had to be gold. But the men had disagreed. Jenny immediately recognized the pellet for what it was. But just to be sure, she soaked it overnight in a pan of caustic potassium carbonate—an acid guaranteed to break up any other metal. The next day she fished out the nugget and, sure enough, it was still whole. After more tests at Sutter's Fort, the nugget was proved beyond doubt to be gold. So that's how one woman started the great California Gold Rush!

# Prospecting

Prospecting for gold isn't something that was done only in the past. You can still prospect for gold today. It's something the whole family can do, it gets you outdoors, it's a quest, and it's great fun. But first you need to know where to look. There are maps that show thousands of sites where gold has been found in the past.

The old prospectors during the California and South Africa gold rushes used different methods to find gold. Sometimes they chipped rock from a rock face and crushed it. Sometimes they sluiced water in a box. But by far the most popular way to find gold cheaply was by panning. And that's what you should plan to do.

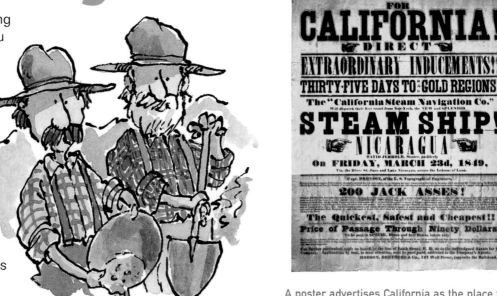

A poster advertises California as the place to go to find gold. It announces that the steam ship *Nicaragua* will be sailing for California on March 23, 1849. The journey there will take just 35 days and the price of a ticket is just $90. The Sutter's Mill discovery had started the Gold Rush!

# Panning

When you've found your stream and located where gold might be found, it's time to get panning.

You'll need:
- a shovel
- a gold pan (which you can buy for around $5 at a hardware store or hobby shop)
- a pair of tweezers
- a small vial into which you put your gold
- a wide-brimmed hat to wear since you will be exposed to the sun

## Fool's Gold

Iron disulfide is a bright golden metal that is often mistaken for gold. It is known as fool's gold. It turns black when given the nitric acid test.

Panning is quite simple. Use the shovel to loosen gravel on the streambed. Then dip the pan into the stream and pick up a little gravel. Swirl the water and gravel around in the pan, allowing gravel to escape. At the base of the pan there might just be a tiny nugget of that heavy, shiny stuff. If you do find a nugget, use the tweezers to pick it up and put it in the vial. Now try again. Good luck!

# Gold mines of the world

Today, gold is excavated from mines on every continent except Antarctica, where mining isn't allowed. Mines can be small or huge, operating underground or in an open pit. It's thought that there are more than 900 mines in operation around the world.

Price increases and the development of new technologies in mining and recovering ore have enabled the development of ore sites that, before now, would have been considered uneconomic. This means far more gold has been mined in the United States, Canada, and Australia than companies thought possible.

Gold has also been produced in countries around the Pacific Rim, in particular Indonesia, which increased its production from 2 tons (1.8 metric tons) in 1992 to 114 tons (103 metric tons) in 2004.

South Africa has produced the most gold over the last 100 years, with the United States and Australia not far behind. In addition, China is coming on strong.

## These are the main gold producing countries:

| Country | Percentage |
| --- | --- |
| South Africa—14% | |
| United States—11% | |
| Australia—10% | |
| China—9% | |
| Russia—7% | |
| Peru—7% | |
| Indonesia—5% | |
| Canada—5% | |
| Other Latin American countries—10% | |
| Other African countries—9% | |
| Rest of world—13% | |

2004 production

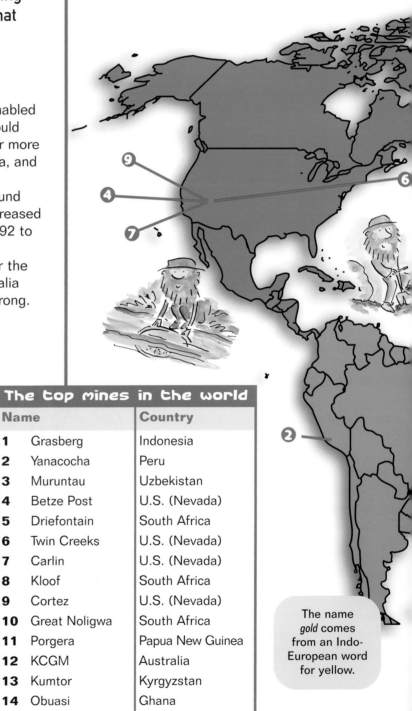

### The top mines in the world

| | Name | Country |
| --- | --- | --- |
| 1 | Grasberg | Indonesia |
| 2 | Yanacocha | Peru |
| 3 | Muruntau | Uzbekistan |
| 4 | Betze Post | U.S. (Nevada) |
| 5 | Driefontain | South Africa |
| 6 | Twin Creeks | U.S. (Nevada) |
| 7 | Carlin | U.S. (Nevada) |
| 8 | Kloof | South Africa |
| 9 | Cortez | U.S. (Nevada) |
| 10 | Great Noligwa | South Africa |
| 11 | Porgera | Papua New Guinea |
| 12 | KCGM | Australia |
| 13 | Kumtor | Kyrgyzstan |
| 14 | Obuasi | Ghana |
| 15 | Sadiola | Mali |

The name *gold* comes from an Indo-European word for yellow.

# Yours or mine?

Who wouldn't like to own a gold mine? Most of us would. But owning a gold mine is not something individuals can do these days. Large companies own most of the gold-producing mines in the world. That's because getting gold out of the ground is a difficult, costly procedure. It costs about $350 to get a single ounce of gold from a mine.

Gold is measured in carats. Originally, a carat was a measure of weight (mass) used by the merchants of the Middle East. It was based on the weight of the carat seed, or bean, which came from the carob bean tree. Carat is now used to determine purity, with 24 carats being pure gold.

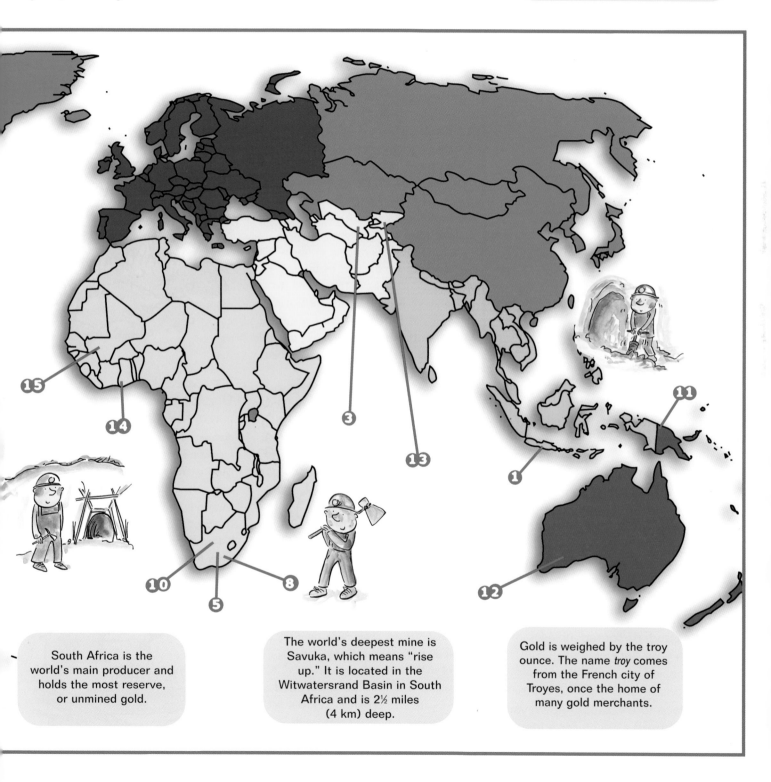

South Africa is the world's main producer and holds the most reserve, or unmined gold.

The world's deepest mine is Savuka, which means "rise up." It is located in the Witwatersrand Basin in South Africa and is 2½ miles (4 km) deep.

Gold is weighed by the troy ounce. The name *troy* comes from the French city of Troyes, once the home of many gold merchants.

# Treasure hunting

Valuable treasure has been buried in the ground since time began. Over the centuries, stories tell of shipwrecked pirates, outlaws, bandits, and rich men buried along with their wealth. These tales may be true, but interesting and valuable finds often lie closer to home. You may have to join a local club and invest in a metal detector to get the best out of this lucrative hobby. But the finds could be worth it!

## Detective stuff!

Serious treasure hunters usually do a lot of research before starting a hunt. They may look at old maps or aerial photos to pinpoint old burial grounds or ancient settlements. They check with local historical societies for old maps of the area or newspaper archives to find out about wealthy individuals who lived nearby. Old tax records could tell if they left the money or buried money, gold, and jewelry in their back yard.

By focusing in on the most likely places, treasure hunters have come up with ancient spears, ax heads, and chisels that are 2,000 years old, plus swords, statues, broaches and, of course, coins.

Begin your hunt close to home—beside old walls or foundations. Pathways are another useful place to try. Most pathways have been used as such for a long time, some for hundreds of years.

Sunken treasure lies scattered over the seabed in many parts of the world. For years, treasure hunters have been diving beneath the waves to investigate ancient shipwrecks, but most of the treasure has never been recovered. Today, modern diving equipment allows divers to stay underwater for hours at a time, and modern metal and sonar detectors make it easier to locate sunken objects.

### The sinking of the Wendela

In 1737, a large ship named the Wendela set sail from the port of Copenhagen in Denmark. The ship was carrying gold coins and bars of silver to be traded for silks, tea, spices, and perfumes in India. As the ship rounded the Shetland Isles north of Scotland, a huge gale blew up. Strong winds and waves drove the ship onto the rocks, where it smashed to pieces and sank. The crew drowned, but pieces of wreckage from the ship washed ashore. Islanders set off with hooks and nets to see what they could salvage.

Only recently has a team of divers been sent out to search for the rest of the Wendela's treasure. They found the rotten wreck encrusted with shells and slimy seaweed, but there were also bags of old silver coins from Holland and Denmark, and gold coins from Spain, buried on the sandy seabed.

### Treasure of Victoria Peak

In 1937, Doc and Ova Noss reportedly discovered some gold bars and other treasure in an abandoned mine in New Mexico. Unfortunately, while they were establishing a claim with the state of New Mexico in 1939, the entrance to the mine collapsed. The bars are supposedly still hidden there—out of reach. Today, the Noss family is still negotiating with the government in its search for the gold.

### Beale Treasure

Thomas Jefferson Beale MAY have buried a vault of gold, silver, and jewels worth tens of millions of dollars in 1819 and 1821 somewhere in Virginia. He disappeared under mysterious circumstances, but not before leaving two coded notes with directions to the treasure. But it's not been found!

# Treasure Island

When Jim Hawkins met a mysterious stranger called Billy at the Admiral Benbow Inn, he was warned to fear a one-legged man. Later, when Billy died of apoplexy, Jim found a map in Billy's old sea chest.

After nearly losing it to a band of pirates, Jim took the map to Squire Trelawney and Doc Livesey, who recognized it as a treasure map showing where Captain Flint, an infamous pirate, had buried his treasure.

The three decided to go and find the treasure and bought a ship called the Hispaniola. The crew was headed by Captain Smollett and included a one-legged cook named Long John Silver.

The night before the ship reached Treasure Island, Jim heard Long John Silver plotting with the crew to kill Smollett, himself, and his friends. He realized that Long John Silver and most of the crew were actually pirates!

Warned of the evil afoot, Captain Smollett sent most of the pirates ashore. Jim decided to go as well, and there he met pirate Ben Gunn, who had been marooned on the island some time before.

Gunn promised to help Jim. Meanwhile, Captain Smollett landed on the island and engaged the pirates in a gun battle.

The pirates won and bargained the lives of the Captain and crew for the treasure map.

But when the treasure was found and the chest opened, it was empty. The pirates turned on Jim, but Ben Gunn told them that he'd dug up the treasure and kept it in his cave.

Did the pirates get the treasure? Find out when you read *Treasure Island*, a great adventure book written by Robert Louis Stevenson. You will enjoy the many twists and turns in the famous story. Happy reading!

# Bullion

## What is bullion?

Bullion is a name for precious metals such as gold, silver, and platinum before they're minted into coins. A precious metal is one that is rare, has a high luster, or shine, and a high melting point. But most importantly, it must be considered valuable, and that depends on its rarity. Bullion is usually found in the shape of blocks or bars called ingots, or it may be minted into bullion coins. All bullion is of a very high purity, although no bullion can be 100 percent pure. Gold can be up to .9999 pure. Unlike money, bullion is valued by its weight and purity.

## Why call it bullion?

The term bullion was first used in the 1300s and probably came from the French word *bouillion*, or boiling. The idea of boiling was probably transferred to melting in English, so a bullion house became a melting house, or mint. The term was properly applied to precious metals in the 1400s.

## Bullion uses today

Today, bullion is used as a trading currency and a commodity across the world. It is also used as an investment because it holds its

## Storing bullion

In order to become wealthy and have something to trade with across the world, countries built up stores of gold and other bullion. It was and is still guarded day and night in the vaults of the world's banks. The $11 billion worth of gold that belongs to the United States is stored at Fort Knox in Kentucky. The vault that contains the bullion is an underground fortress with concrete, bomb-proof walls and lots of alarms. Eight countries store their bullion at the Federal Reserve Bank of New York, making it the biggest hoard of bullion in the world.

value well over long periods of time. Bullion is often seen as a hedge, or safe bet, against inflation or a downward turn in the economy.

## Alchemy

In the Middle Ages, people tried to make gold from less valuable metals. This science was called alchemy. The alchemists mixed gold with metals and powders, stirred and heated it, and sometimes even muttered a few spells over the mixture, hoping it would turn to pure gold! Some alchemists were serious scientists, but others were really magicians or frauds who sold fake gold. As alchemists tried one experiment after another, they discovered new facts about gold and other metals. They learned how to clean and purify them, how to mix them together to make strong alloys, and how to mold and decorate them. Eventually laws were passed to stop fake gold being made, so many alchemists went out of business. Modern scientists have tried to manufacture gold, too, but so far they haven't been successful either!

## Bullion holders

- United States
- Germany
- International Monetary Fund
- France
- Switzerland
- Italy

# The gold standard

For thousands of years, gold has been the standard of value; a base against which to measure currency. This helped countries trade with each other. A country was on the gold standard when it could convert its money into gold if required and when it agreed to buy or sell gold at a fixed price. By 1900 all leading countries were using the gold standard to trade with each other.

## One speck of gold before meals!

For thousands of years, gold dust has been mixed with medicines and given to patients suffering from all kinds of illnesses. Doctors in ancient China mixed an elixir, or "miracle cure," which contained gold dust. Modern scientists are working on several cures using gold. It is possible that gold can cure aches and pains, such as arthritis. This painful illness is caused when the joints of the body become swollen and stiff. Many people have gold inside their mouths. Because gold does not stain or rust and can be shaped easily, it is sometimes used to make false teeth and fillings. Fine gold wire helps to keep the teeth in position in the mouth while the dentist is at work.

## Gold reserves

Today gold plays little part in world monetary systems. Money is based on the value of the American dollar and not on the stocks of valuable gold bullion stored around the world. It is still a very valuable metal, but the enormous hoards of gold amassed by governments under the gold standard now lie in storage, gathering dust. All told, banks and governments hold more than 30,000 tons of gold—the amount that could be mined in 13 years. Another 10 years' worth of mine production is stored as bars and coins in the hoards of private investors and a further 25 years' worth as jewelry.

In the 1980s, as more and more mines opened around the world, stocks started to pile high and the value of gold began to fall. Today, it's worth only about one-quarter of what it was when its price peaked in 1980. And as the price of gold declines, governments are rethinking their stockpiles. The central banks of the United Kingdom, the Netherlands, Belgium, Canada, Argentina, and Australia have all sold significant stocks of gold. Surprisingly, Switzerland, the third-largest national reserve of gold in the world, now plans to sell some of its treasure.

# The assay office

Once gold has been cleaned of rock, dust, and other metals, it must be assayed, or tested, to find out how pure it is. The assayist rubs the gold sample against a lump of hard, black rock called a touchstone. He tests the tiny sample left on the touchstone with a drop of nitric acid. Pure gold does not mark or tarnish, but poorer quality gold will show an acid stain.

Its quality is measured in carats. Pure gold is 24 carats and is too soft to use. Gold that is 22 carats contains other metals that make it tougher. It can then be molded into rings and other jewelry. Gold that is nine carats is less valuable but keeps its shape well. It is sometimes used to make pen nibs.

# Marco Polo
## and the silk notes

Marco Polo was an Italian voyager and merchant. He was one of the first Europeans to travel across Asia. After a three-year journey, he finally arrived in China in 1274. There he was greeted by the great Mongol emperor Kublai Khan, who invited him to explore his kingdom.

Polo saw many wondrous things, but the thing that puzzled him the most was the Chinese custom of buying goods with nothing more than a few pieces of paper.

Whereas Europe was still trading with coins, the Chinese had been using notes, or paper money, since the 11th century.

Originally, the Chinese called their notes flying money because they were so light they could easily be blown out of the holder's hands.

In addition, the Chinese had long introduced a system of credit. A merchant could deposit money in the capital and get a paper certificate that he could exchange in the provinces.

The notes that Marco Polo came across were called silk notes. The Mongols had issued them when they came to power in China, and the value that supported the notes wasn't gold or silver, as it might be today, but bundles of silk yarn.

Marco Polo was so impressed, he wrote a detailed description of how the notes were made using etched copper print plates, and how the money was then issued with great solemnity and authority.

Every note bore the names and seals of several officials, so they were difficult to forge. In China, forgery was punishable by death.

# Old notes

Cloth banknote for three strings of cash, from China, 1933

Banknote for 100 dalers, Sweden, 1666

100 strang note, from Tibet, 1940s

Confederate $500 note issued during the U.S. Civil War

Assignat note for 50 sols, France, 1793

# Paper money

When goldsmiths started creating paper money, they probably didn't realize how important it would become. Today it's the money we carry around with us, the stuff that takes up room in our wallets. You can't take a paper note to the bank any longer and expect to have it replaced by a lump of gold, but it is still considered to have value—simply because everyone agrees that it can be used to buy things.

The banknote, or paper money, is issued by the main banking authority in the country in which it is issued. The Bank of England issues it in the United Kingdom, for example, while the Federal Reserve Bank issues it in the United States. The money is then distributed to the commercial banks. Each bank must keep a reserve of banknotes, with a limit set by the government. This makes sure that a bank always has enough paper money to pay its customers should they ask for it.

Banknotes are issued in what are called denominations. These state the value of the money. The U.S. dollar is issued in ones, twos, fives, 10s, 20s, 50s, and 100s.

The average life of a banknote depends on its size. The larger ones last longer than the small ones. Once notes become ragged or torn, new bank notes are printed to replace old ones as they wear out.

Buying a wife with tobacco leaves!

## Tobacco money

In the 1600s, tobacco became the main crop grown by colonists in North America. It soon became so important and valuable that it took over from gold and silver as the monetary standard. It was often called country money or country pay. Clergymen, for example, were paid in tobacco until 1758.

Tobacco was also used to buy things—and people. For example, 60 future wives arrived in the colony of Virginia in 1621 and sold to settlers for 150 pounds of tobacco each. As well as tobacco itself, tobacco notes, which vouched for the quality and quantity of tobacco in public warehouses, were authorized as legal tender in Virginia in the early 1700s.

## The greenback

The greenback is the nickname for the U.S. one dollar bill. The name came from the green color of the note itself. Today we only think of greenbacks in terms of an ordinary dollar, but in the early days of the United States the term greenback was negative.

The currency was issued by the U.S. Treasury, in part, to finance the Civil War. It was "fiat money," or money by government decree, so it couldn't be redeemed for gold. The greenback era ended in 1879, but the name has stuck.

# Designing notes

Since banknotes are a form of money, they have to be made so that people can't forge them easily. There's a lot of secrecy about how a banknote is actually produced. We are, however, allowed to know the general process that creates the money in your wallet!

## Design

The first step in the process is design. An artist creates a design, then perfects it on a screen using a computer program. Colors are decided on and the different printing colors are separated, also on a computer. Then lithograph plates are made.

## Papermaking

Any old paper won't do for a banknote. You don't want the note tearing or falling apart after a few days' use. For security, notes are printed on paper that's made from cotton fibers. The paper also contains a special kind of thread that can't be photocopied.

## Intaglio

The artist's design is engraved onto a steel plate, called an intaglio plate. The engraver uses sharp tools, called burins, and a magnifying glass to do this work, which often takes several weeks. When ink is applied to a plate, it fills in the lines and marks of the engraver's design. The inked plate is then pressed onto the paper to give an impression, or raised print, of the design.

## Printing

The background design is printed using offset lithography, a system where the design is separated into three groups of colors—already done by the computer. The inks are transferred onto a rubber-covered cylinder that combines the colors and prints the image. Letterpress, a different kind of printing, is used to print official signatures and to add a different serial number to each note.

## Security

Specially mixed inks are used to apply invisible, secret security features onto each bank note. Today, even more sophisticated inks have been developed that only show up under ultraviolet light.

## Checking

Checking means that banks and stores can use special lights to detect forgeries. Most notes have a watermark design that is molded into the paper. It can be seen when you hold up a note to the light. Often the security thread appears and disappears between the bars of the watermark. Green and red security threads make banknotes impossible to photocopy because the thread just looks black when photocopied.

# Forgery

Because paper money and coins are so important to trade and to the prosperity of a country, it is really important that coins and notes aren't forged. In the past, the punishment for forgery has been high. Until the early 1830s, forgery carried the death penalty in England. That meant it was considered just as bad as murder.

## The art of forgery

To create a forgery is to make an exact fake or counterfeit of something. Bank notes and coins can be forged. So can paintings and other things, such as signatures on documents and legal papers. But the most important thing is that the forger must intend to deceive, or cheat, someone by making the forgery. A copy, replica, or reproduction of something isn't a forgery, unless you try to convince someone it's the real thing.

Counterfeit money is usually paper that has been printed to look like banknotes. There are elements within a banknote, such as watermarks, that make it difficult to counterfeit. But modern technology has made forgery easier. Some forgers use a graphic art camera and filter. Color copiers and computer printers are also used, but the counterfeits aren't as realistic.

## Famous forgery

The best-known forgeries are of artwork. A Dutch painter called Han van Meegeren forged a number of Vermeer paintings just after World War II that even fooled the experts.

And the great Michelangelo himself forged a sleeping cupid sculpture that he aged in the ground to make it look old. He sold it to a Roman Catholic cardinal, who found out about it later on but never got his money back!

Will your winning banknote design bring you fame and fortune?

## Old and new

All banknotes wear out in time. They are taken out of circulation as they begin to look tired.

What is the life span of a banknote? Look on the phone screen to see just what a short life a banknote can have!

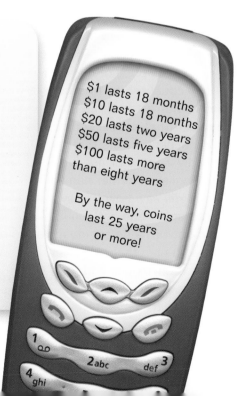

$1 lasts 18 months
$10 lasts 18 months
$20 lasts two years
$50 lasts five years
$100 lasts more than eight years

By the way, coins last 25 years or more!

# Stamps

Because stamps are usually worth a certain amount of money, they can be used as a form of currency. A stamp that has 37 cents written on it is worth 37 cents, so you could trade it for 37 cents. Once it's been used, however, it loses its value. But not always. Some stamps are so valuable they can fetch millions of dollars today. But how did ordinary stamps come to exist? Well, it's all part of the postal system, which began long ago.

## The mail system

Some historians believe that the Persian monarch King Cyrus established the first troop of mail couriers as long ago as 550 B.C. The Romans also had a sophisticated postal system with staging places called *mansio posita*, from which our word *post* comes. However, when the Roman Empire collapsed, the postal system went with it and it wasn't until the Middle Ages that organized courier systems were started again.

At first only official letters were sent, but soon private letters were sent as well. It was an expensive business, however, and not always efficient. The recipient of the letter had to pay the price of delivery, and they could refuse to accept it if they couldn't afford the cost. This meant that people sometimes couldn't accept letters that they very badly wanted or needed.

An English reformer named Rowland Hill saw how this system could be unfair and set about coming up with a better idea. He proposed a plan that called for preprinted envelopes and adhesive postage stamps: a "bit of paper just large enough to bear the stamp and covered at the back

Early postmen collected the charges.

with a glutinous wash," as he described it in a letter addressed to the government. He also proposed that the cost should be a penny per half-ounce a letter, which was affordable to most. His idea was accepted, and on May 1, 1840, the world's first stamp went on sale. The Penny Black, as it was called, bore the head of Queen Victoria, and, like all stamps that came afterward, enabled people to prepay for postage based on the weight of the letter.

The Penny Black was the first stamp in the world to be issued. A used one is worth more than $125, while one in mint condition is worth $3,500.

## Stamps today

Modern stamps are issued by a post office, affiliated with the government, and come in many different denominations and designs. (In England, for example, every design has to be examined by the queen.)

The background of the stamp is usually complicated so that it's not easy to forge. After printing, the stamps are sent in sheets to post offices or other outlets. Once a stamp has been used, it's canceled with an indelible ink so that it can't be used again.

## Making stamps

Before a stamp can be made, it has to be designed. Specialized stamp designers do this. They are used to working in very fine and miniscule detail. Interestingly, in the United States you can't put the head of any living person on a stamp. Once a design has been agreed on a plate is engraved with the picture. Initially, flat plates were used, but today most are curved or cylindrical. Inside the printing press a cylinder is inked and the ink transferred to the paper. Sheets of stamps are then sent to the post office. Rolls of stamps are made for stamp machines, and booklets for retail sales.

# Stamp collections

Ever since countries began issuing stamps, people have collected them. Philately, or stamp collecting, is still one of the world's great hobbies. The first philatelic society was founded in 1865 in France. One of its founders, Georges Herpin, coined the word *philately* from two Greek words, *phila*, which means "to love," and *ateles*, which means "free of charge."

Stamp collecting is fun because it can be inexpensive and anyone can do it. In fact, some countries produce stamps that are intended just for collectors rather than for postal use. All you need is an idea of what kind of stamp you want to collect. Some people collect transport stamps, others rare stamps, or stamps with animals on them. Your collection can be personal to you.

# Your stamp collection

One of the first things to remember when starting out is that stamps are delicate and have to be handled carefully.

- Wash your hands before handling them.
- Keep them away from food and drink.
- Keep them out of direct sunlight to prevent fading.

## Storing

You will need a magnifying glass and a stamp album or glassine envelopes.

## Stamp hinges

Stamp hinges are designed so that stamps can be fixed to a page and taken off again without damaging them. Don't use sticky tape or glue to fix stamps or you'll never be able to remove them or sell them. Buy stamps in good condition, rather than cheap or damaged ones. Creases and tears always reduce the value of a stamp.

## Stamp tongs

Special tweezers with flattened ends are used to pick up stamps. Tweezers keep the grease and oil from your hands off the stamps.

## Removing stamps

Always remove stamps from their backing by soaking them in water. If you try to peel them off, you'll probably tear them. Once removed, dry stamps on a flat surface, on a paper towel. Soak stamps with magenta cancellation ink separately, because these inks can run and spoil other stamps. Get the stamp out of the water as soon as the ink begins to run.

## Counterfeits

Like money, stamps can be counterfeited, and it takes an expert to spot a forgery. Some stamps may look good, but have been repaired. If you hold a stamp up to bright light, you can often spot the repair marks.

# Famous stamps

Here are a few famous stamps collectors would love to own:

### Inverted Jenny

This U.S. postal stamp issued in 1918 has the aircraft in the middle printed upside down. About 100 were found. It's worth more than $100,000.

### Treskilling yellow

A Swedish issue is the most valuable stamp in the world. In 1855, when Sweden issued its first postage stamps, the 3-skilling issue was supposed to be blue-green in color. The 8-skilling issue was orangish yellow. Somehow, one or more (no one knows how many) 3-skilling stamps were printed in the yellow color. No one seemed to notice. Then, in 1886, a collector named Georg Baeckman found the stamp in his grandma's attic and sold it to a dealer for 7 kroner (about $1). Through the years, the rare and possibly only surviving stamp has passed through several different hands. In 1996, it was sold again for $2.2 million.

### British Guiana 1 cent magenta

Issued in 1856, the rare "black on magenta" stamp features a sailing ship and the motto of its country. Only one now exists. Millionaire John E. duPont bought it for $935,000 in 1980. It's now locked away in a safe, while its owner serves 30 years for murder!

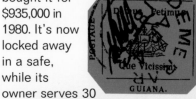

# Checks

Long before checks were thought about, the goldsmiths who forged gold coins began to offer a new service. They would hold other people's gold in their safes for security. They then issued notes, or receipts, to say that they would pay back the gold when the customers wanted it.

But two important things happened. First, few people wanted their gold back—it was safer with the goldsmith; and second, everyone started swapping the notes to buy things instead of using their gold. This meant that both gold and notes were circulating in society and being used as money. In fact, the goldsmiths had invented a new kind of money, in the form of a valuable paper receipt. Soon everybody was using the receipts and not the gold itself.

The goldsmiths soon realized that they could create as many receipts as they wanted, as long as no one asked for their gold back.

## Checks

The idea of the check began during a war that took place in England in the 1600s. Wealthy people, afraid they might lose their possessions, put gold, jewelry, and coins into goldsmiths' safes to protect them. Sometimes they would give written instructions to the goldsmiths to use these goods to pay someone else. These instructions were the first checks. They were like the goldsmiths' receipts that eventually became banknotes.

Checks didn't come into general use, though, until the late 1800s. A check is a written order by an account holder to pay a sum of money to the bearer (of the check) or a named recipient. A check is not in itself legal tender. It is, however, a legal document.

# Money orders

Just like a check, a money order is a device for making payments. It looks a little like a check or banknote and it has a value of whatever denomination you choose. When you buy a money order from a company, you pay the amount plus a charge on top of that. The name of the person you wish to pay is put on the money order, and it can then be used to pay bills, add to a current account, or buy goods and services.

# What's new with checks?

Changes have been brewing in the way banks handle checks. The Check 21 system, which is short for the Check Clearing for the 21st Century Act, went into effect in late 2004. It speeds up the time it takes for banks to process and clear checks.

## Here's how it works

John receives a bill in the mail for his electricity use. He writes a check to the power company and drops it off at the post office.

## Your own design

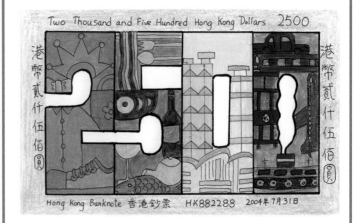

### Design a banknote

In a competition organized by the Hong Kong Heritage Museum and the HSBC bank, young artists and designers were asked to create a design for a Hong Kong banknote. The theme was "Bank Notes that Tell a Story." Wong Cheuk Hin, 11, designed the winning entry in the children's section. He used the four basic necessities of life—clothing, housing, food, and transportation—in his design. The judges were looking for originality, creativity, and a feeling for Hong Kong's bustling character. Wong Cheuk Hin, who likes painting and wants to be an artist in the future, hit the mark with his work, which was put on display at the Hong Kong Heritage Museum.

Wong Cheuk Hin with his winning note

### Old way

In the old system, the check would pass through various local and regional banks before finally ending up at John's bank.

### New way

In the Check 21 system, the check can be scanned electronically by any bank along the way. The bank would then destroy the paper copy so there aren't two copies of the same check. Then, the electronic image is sent to John's bank. However, if John's bank still wants to receive a paper copy of the check, the bank can issue a substitute check.

### What's a substitute check?

A substitute check is a paper copy of the electronic image of the original check. It contains the same information as the original check, and it can be used in the same way as the original. There is a statement printed on every substitute check to make sure the document is not forged. If the statement is not present, John's bank could not accept it. If the statement is on the substitute check, it can be processed, and John's bill is paid.

This new law does not require banks to exchange the electronically scanned checks or produce substitute checks. However, it does require that banks accept substitute checks from other banks.

# Plastic money

You may hear someone say, when they're going to buy a snazzy pair of shoes they've just seen, "Oh, don't worry, I'll just use plastic." You know what they mean, but does it really feel as if the plastic they're talking about —the store card or credit card— is real money? Just because cash doesn't get passed across the counter, it doesn't mean you're not paying. The paying part may be delayed slightly, but it will happen. And, if you use a credit card, you'll probably end up paying more than just the cost of the new shoes.

## The ATM

The first automated teller machine, or ATM, was devised by a Turkish inventor named Luther George Simjian in 1939. The first ATM was installed in a Citicorp Bank in New York, but lasted just six months, because the only people who used it were a few gamblers who didn't want to deal with tellers face-to-face.

The modern ATM was the brainchild of Don Wetzel, who came up with the idea while he was waiting in line at a bank in Dallas. It took $5 million before Wetzel and his group came up with the right machine, which was installed in the New York Chemical Bank.

By 1973, 2,000 ATMs operated in the United States. Today there are nearly 400,000 ATMs in the United States.

## What is credit?

Credit simply means giving someone time to pay. So when you sell something to someone and they promise to pay you back later, you're giving them credit. The word credit comes from the Latin word *credere*, which means "trust." So when you give someone time to pay, you trust they'll pay you back. Usually, the person giving credit will make a small charge, normally a percentage of the total, to be paid each month or year until the money is repaid. This fee is called interest.

### The rise of credit

Ancient civilizations, such as Assyria, Babylon, and Egypt, all used a kind of credit, even when bartering. But credit became really popular in the 1100s, when fairs were more common and people traveled greater distances to buy and sell things. They used credit to buy goods in one place, sold them at a profit in another place, and then paid back the credit with part of the profit after that. Payment by installment was introduced later.

### Paying back in installments

One of the first types of credit agreement used by ordinary people was a secured loan called hire purchase. Under that system, a finance company bought the product for you, perhaps a car or a domestic appliance you couldn't afford to buy outright, and you paid the company back over so many months or years. This was a secure form of credit since the company could take back the product if you failed to pay. Today, laws protect people using finance agreements and make sure they're aware of what they're agreeing to.

### PINs

A Personal Identification Number, or PIN, is a number that is special to you and which allows you to use a plastic card to get money out of an ATM. After keying in your PIN number, the modern ATM offers a list of services, including cash withdrawal and statement updates.

# The credit card

Credit cards first came into use in the 1950s, when organizations such as Diners Club and American Express offered a form of unsecured credit. In other words, it wasn't backed up by any product or property. These cards evolved from shoppers' plates, a kind of store card used in the 1920s that could only be used in stores. Store cards, or charge cards, which could be used in a single store or chain only, allowed their customers to buy on credit and pay later.

Bank credit cards followed. Bank of America launched the BankAmericard (now VISA) so card-holders could buy from any approved place and pay later. Today, credit is available to almost anyone, and that's mainly because of the growth of plastic money.

## Debit cards

Debit cards are used at point-of-sale areas. They came into use in 1985, and there are now millions of point-of-sale terminals around the world. A debit card looks just like a credit card and is used as an alternative to cash. Today there are two different types of debit card, online and offline. An online card requires a PIN that is used at the point-of-sale terminal. A separate keypad is needed to allow the customer to select the account from which money will be drawn.

Offline cards carry the logo of a credit card company, such as Visa or Mastercard. There is usually a daily limit on how much cash can be spent.

## Store cards

Store cards are credit cards you can use only in the stores that issue them. Interest rates are generally very high, which make the cards expensive if you don't pay them off right away.

## Cards just for you!

There are now new kinds of cards specially designed for young people to use. They're purchased by parents and have an established credit total. You can use these up to the credit limit—then, of course, you have to negotiate with your parents to increase your card's purchase power!

## Smart card

How we pay for things is changing rapidly and will continue to change. Credit card information, for example, may be kept in a single smart card. So you won't have a wallet full of different cards, just one. All the relevant information will be downloaded into the computer chip embedded in the card.

## Credit card & identity theft

Few crooks actually steal cards these days. It's too easy for the card-holders to call their credit company and report it. A much better scam is to get personal details about someone and use these to run up huge overdrafts and loan amounts before the owner catches on.

Identity theft, which is the theft of personal data, is growing as more and more people use cards instead of checks. Between 1998 and 2003, 27.3 million Americans suffered from this kind of theft. In just one year, it has cost business $48 billion in losses, and consumers $5 billion in personal losses.

Most often identity theft is an inside job. Employees in a business that has access to customer information steal huge amounts of data and records. This information can then be sold to criminals for $5 to $10 per record or credit report.

Another scam is called phishing. The phisher sends large numbers of e-mails to addresses, asking the recipient to reply with personal financial data. Up to 5 percent respond to these e-mails that might be about 'changes to an account,' or something similar.

# International money

What happens when you come across a coin or banknote that's been issued in a different country? Is it still money? Yes, it certainly is, because it can buy things in the country in which it was issued. It can also be used to buy other currencies. So if you were given Japanese yen, for example, you could use them to buy dollars or pounds or any other currency. This is called currency exchange. Here are a few of the currencies that you might come across on your world travels.

## Euro

The euro is a common currency, one used by more than one country. The euro, as legal tender, came into existence in 1999, and is used by the 12 countries of the European Union. Each coin carries a European design on one side and a national design on the other. Euros are divided into 100 cents.

## Rand

The rand is the official currency of South Africa. It was first used in 1961 to replace the South African pound. The coin was named after the Witwatersrand gold mining area. A new R5 coin was minted in 2004 to stop forgeries. Now coins have security features of micro-lettering and bimetal design.

## Czech koruna

The official currency of the Czech Republic is the koruna, or crown. It is used in both the Czech Republic and Slovakia.

## Swiss franc

The Swiss franc is the only franc currency still used in Europe. It is the currency of Switzerland and Liechtenstein. Coins range from 1 centime to 5 francs. Because Switzerland is divided into three language areas, the currency is called a franc in the French speaking area, a franken in the German speaking area, and a franco in the Italian speaking area.

## Australian dollar

The Australian dollar is the official currency of the Commonwealth of Australia and is sometimes affectionately called the Aussie Battler. The dollar is divided into 100 cents, with coins ranging from 5 cents up to five dollars. The currency was first used in 1966.

## Barbados dollar

The national currency of Barbados is the Barbados dollar, which is divided into 100 cents. It was created by the Central Bank of Barbados and is pegged to the U.S. dollar. Before that, Barbados used the Eastern Caribbean dollar. Many of the country's coins are made at the Royal Canadian Mint.

## Singapore dollar

The official currency of Singapore, the Singapore dollar, uses the symbol S$ so people can tell it from all the other dollars. All coins from one cent to one dollar feature a flower on one side and the Singapore coat of arms on the other.

# Foreign exchange

Right up to the 1900s, nobody thought about making money by buying foreign currency in the hope it would become more valuable than their own. After all, most currencies were pegged to the price of gold—the gold standard—that had the same value all over the world.

## Gold standard to dollar standard

But after World War I, things changed and speculation grew almost tenfold. It started as one country after another moved away from the gold standard. And things became even more unsettled after World War II. Up to that time, the British pound had been the world's main currency, but the war changed all that and now it was the U.S. dollar.

Delegates from 44 countries met at Bretton Woods, New Hampshire, and agreed to peg their currencies to the U.S. dollar. So if the dollar bought two pounds in England, for instance, it couldn't buy more than £2.02 or less than £1.98 before the Central Bank would step in to bring the currency into line. At the same time, the dollar was pegged to gold at $35 an ounce. This made all the currencies stable for a time.

## Floating

But the agreement didn't last. Many European countries didn't want to be tied to the dollar. They wanted a free-floating system that allowed their currencies to "float," or move in any direction, regardless of what was happening to other currencies. That is what happens today.

### Foreign currencies

| Name | Country | Name | Country |
|------|---------|------|---------|
| Argentina | Peso | Haiti | Gourde |
| Australia | Dollar | Iraq | Dinar |
| Bahrain | Dinar | Japan | Yen |
| Brazil | Real | Malaysia | Ringgit |
| Canada | Dollar | Mexico | Peso |
| Chile | Peso | New Zealand | Dollar |
| Congo | Franc | Peru | New Sol |
| Georgia | Lari | Saudi Arabia | Riyal |
| Guatemala | Quetzal | South Korea | Won |

# Getting your hands on foreign money

If you're going on a vacation to a foreign country, you'll need to buy foreign money. For instance, if you're going to France you'll need euros, if you're going to Mexico you'll need pesos, and if you're going to China you'll need yuan.

You can buy foreign currency at a bank or at an agency such as American Express. Each seller will charge a fee for making the exchange, which might be a small percentage of the total, with a minimum amount per transaction.

You should compare exchange rates used by different outlets, because different companies can use higher or lower rates. Be aware as well that exchange rates are different when you buy foreign money compared to when you sell it.

You'll always get a better rate when you buy. Money changers usually give both rates. It's best to get rid of all your foreign money before you return home from abroad, because no one at home really wants it that badly, and you won't get the best exchange rate for it.

# Traveler's checks

When James Fargo, the president of American Express, traveled abroad in the late 1800s, he found to his embarrassment that he couldn't get his U.S. checks cashed in Europe. Upset by this, he asked an employee, Marcellus Berry, to solve the problem. Berry thought up the traveler's check in 1891.

### Just imagine

You've just got to your vacation destination and you're about to enjoy your first ice cream on the beach. You put your hand in your bag or pocket to pull out your wallet—and you freeze. The wallet's not there. It's been stolen. Your vacation is ruined. Never fear, there's a solution—the traveler's check.

American Express was the first company to offer the checks. For a fee, you buy the checks in dollars or pounds or another currency. Traveler's checks come in different denominations, but always a fixed amount, and they're made out to you. You sign in front of the teller for each check. You cash the checks at an exchange company or bank for the relevant value, and you sign in front of the teller to prove it's you who's doing the cashing and not a thief.

# Glossary

### abacus
An abacus is a device that was invented thousands of years ago for counting and doing arithmetic.

### alchemy
Alchemy was the practice of trying to make gold from other metals.

### assay
An assay is a test carried out on a metal object to see what it contains. It is used to test gold and silver coins and bullion.

### asset
An asset is an item of value owned by a person or a business.

### ATM (automated teller machine)
An ATM is a machine that can issue money from a bank account.

### auction
An auction is a form of public sale where goods are offered for sale without a given price. Each is sold to the person who offers most.

### aureus
An aureus was a gold coin used in Roman times.

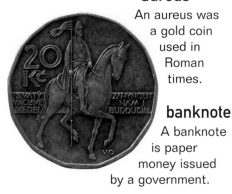

### banknote
A banknote is paper money issued by a government.

### Bank of England
The Bank of England is the central bank of the United Kingdom.

### Barbary Corsair
The Barbary Corsairs were pirates who plundered ships off the coast of North Africa in the 1500s.

### barter
To barter is to trade goods or services without using money.

### bullion
Bullion is bars of gold or silver before they are made into coins.

### carat
A carat is the standard measurement of the purity of a piece of gold.

### check
A check is a printed piece of paper that orders a bank to pay money out of a customer's account.

### commodity
A commodity is goods like grain, gold, or oil, that is traded in the belief that it will be worth more later, so it can be sold for a profit.

### cowrie shell
Cowrie shells are seashells that were once used like coins to barter or exchange goods.

### credit
Credit is an arrangement a customer can make to pay for goods later on.

### credit card
A credit card is a plastic card used to buy goods and services to be paid for at a later date.

### cuneiform
Cuneiform was an early form of writing using wedge-shaped marks scratched into clay.

### currency
Currency is the money used by a particular country.

### debit
A debit is a loss or expense recorded in a company's account books.

### debit card
A debit card is a plastic card that is used like a check to pay for goods. It promises to pay for the goods out of your bank account.

### denarius
A denarius was a silver coin used in Roman times.

### denomination
A denomination is the value printed on the face of a coin or bank note.

### double-entry bookkeeping
Double-entry bookkeeping describes the way that transactions are recorded in two columns, those that earn money and spend money.

### drachma
The drachma is the currency of Greece.

### ducat
Ducat was the name given to several kinds of gold and silver coins used in Europe in the past.

### economy

The economy of a country is everything to do with the way it produces things and sells them.

### euro
The euro is the currency used in most countries of the European Union.

### exchange rate
The exchange rate shows how much a currency is worth when it's changed into another currency.

### Federal Reserve
The Federal Reserve is the central bank of the United States.

### finance company
A finance company provides money to people and companies that wish to borrow money.

### florin
A florin was a gold coin originally used in Florence, Italy, in the 1200s. Other European countries also used this name for their coins.

### fool's gold
Fool's gold is a familiar name for the mineral iron sulphide, which is sometimes mistaken for gold.

### foreign exchange
Foreign exchange is the buying and selling of world currencies.

### forgery
A forgery is something that is made to look like something else, usually with the intention of cheating people.

### Fort Knox
Fort Knox is one of the largest vaults used by the Federal Reserve to store its bullion.

### galleon
A galleon was a large sailing ship used in the 1500s.

### gold standard
The gold standard was a system used in the past to fix the value of a currency to the value of an ounce of gold.

### goldsmith
A goldsmith is a person who makes objects out of gold.

### greenback
Greenback is a familiar term used to describe the green dollar note of the United States.

### hallmark
A hallmark is a set of symbols stamped on an object made of gold, silver, or platinum.

### hire purchase
Hire purchase describes the system of buying goods in installments over a period of time.

### identity theft
Identity theft is the practice of stealing personal details belonging to someone in order to steal money from their account.

### Inca
The Inca were an Indian civilization that once lived in the Andes Mountains of South America.

### income tax
Income tax is the tax paid by people to the government as a percentage of their earnings.

### inflation
Inflation is a rise in prices caused when there is too much money in circulation and not enough goods and services.

### ingot
An ingot is another name for a block or bar of metal.

### installment
An installment is a part payment for goods or services supplied.

### interest
Interest is a charge made for a loan of money.

### krone
The krone is the currency of several countries, including Denmark and Norway.

## legal tender
Legal tender means coins and notes that can be used to buy things.

## liability
Liability is an amount of money that a person owes to another.

## measure of value
A measure of value is any form of money that has a fixed value.

## milling
Milling is the pattern of small grooves around the edge of some coins.

## mohur
The mohur is a small coin once used in India.

## money order
A money order is a form that promises to pay a certain amount of money on demand.

## overdraft
An overdraft is a form of loan made by a bank to its customers.

## philately
Philately describes the hobby of collecting postage stamps.

## pictograph
A pictograph was an ancient form of communication using a set of drawn symbols scratched in clay.

## PIN (personal identification number)
A PIN is a private number code issued to a debit or credit card holder to enable them to draw funds or buy goods using their card.

## potlatch
Potlatch was a ceremonial feast held by Northwest Coast Indians when a chief's wealth was shown and shared with his tribe.

## pound
The pound is the currency of several countries of the world, including Lebanon, Syria, and the United Kingdom.

## profit
Profit is the money earned when income is greater than expenditure.

## quipu
A quipu was a set of colored strings with knots, used for counting and recording the date in ancient Peru.

## reale
A reale is a silver coin that was once used in Spain and its colonies.

## rupee
The rupee is the currency of several countries of the world, including India, Pakistan, and Sri Lanka.

## sestertius
A sestertius was a bronze coin used in Roman times that bore the head of the Roman Emperor.

## smart card
A single smart card can replace all of a person's credit cards to make spending easier.

## store card
A store card is a form of credit card issued by a shop or store.

## tally
A tally was a stick cut with notches to represent sums of money due as taxes.

## tax
Tax is the money paid by people and companies to the government to help fund the running of the country.

## thaler
The thaler was a German coin used many years ago, which gave its name to the dollar.

## Third World debt
Third World debt describes the large sums of money owed by poor countries to rich countries, which, in many cases, cannot be repaid.

## touchstone
A touchstone was a piece of schist or quartz rock used in olden days to test the purity of a coin.

## traveler's check
A traveler's check is a form of money order that can be exchanged for currencies abroad.

## wampum
A wampum is a collection of shell beads once used in barter by North American Indians.

## yen
The yen is the currency of Japan.

## yuan
The yuan is the currency of China.

# Want to Learn More?

## At the Library

Bateman, Katherine R. *The Young Investor: Projects and Activities for Making Your Money Grow.* Chicago: Chicago Review Press, 2001.

Godfrey, Neale S. *Neale S. Godfrey's Ultimate Kids' Money Book.* New York: Simon & Schuster Books for Young Readers, 1998.

Harman, Hollis Page. *Money Sense for Kids!* 2nd ed. Hauppauge, N.Y.: Barron's, 2004.

Otfinoski, Steven. *The Kids' Guide to Money: Earning It, Saving It, Spending It, Growing It, Sharing It.* New York: Scholastic, 1996.

## Look for all the books in this series:

Common Cents
*The Money in Your Pocket*
0-7565-1671-4

Cowries, Coins, Credit
*The History of Money*
0-7565-1676-5

Get Rich Quick?
*Earning Money*
0-7565-1674-9

Money: It's Our Job
*Money Careers*
0-7565-1675-7

Save, Spend, Share
*Using Your Money*
0-7565-1672-2

What's It All Worth?
*The Value of Money*
0-7565-1673-0

## On the Web

For more information on *the history of money,* use FactHound to track down Web sites related to this book.

1. Go to *www.facthound.com*
2. Type in a search word related to this book or this book ID: 0756516765
3. Click on the *Fetch It* button.
FactHound will fetch the best Web sites for you!

# Index

abacus, 13
adversaria, 13
alchemy, 28
Alexander the Great, 7, 9
Ambrosiana Library, 15
American Express, 39, 41
animals, 6, 7, 8, 12
annealing furnaces, 15
assaying, 29
Atahualpa (Inca emperor), 20
Australian dollar, 40
authenticity, 14
automated teller machines (ATMs), 38
Aztecs, 6

Baeckman, Georg, 35
bank notes, 7
Bank of America, 39
Bank of Barcelona, 6
Bank of England, 15, 31
Bank of North America, 7
BankAmericard, 39
banknotes, 31, 32, 33, 36, 37
banks, 7, 28, 31, 36, 37
Barbados dollar, 40
Barbarossa, 21
Barbary Corsairs, 21
bartering, 8, 38
Beale, Thomas Jefferson, 26
Berry, Marcellus, 41
Blackbeard. *See* Teach, Edward.
blanking presses, 15
blanks, 15
bookkeeping, 12, 13
booty, 20
British Guiana 1 cent magenta stamp, 35
British pounds, 41
bronze, 8, 10
buccaneers, 20
bullion, 28, 29
burins, 32

Caesar, Julius, 7
carat seeds, 25
carats, 25, 29
cashbooks, 13
Central Bank of Barbados, 40
cents, 15
Check 21 system, 36-37
checking, 32
checks, 7, 36-37
Cheng I, 21
Cheng I Sao, 21

circulation, 33
Citicorp Bank, 38
Civil War, 31
cleaning, 15, 16
codex accepti et expensi, 13
Codex Atlanticus (Leonardo da Vinci), 15
coin collections, 16-17
coin detectors, 17
coin sizers, 15
coining presses, 15
coins, 8, 9, 10, 13, 14, 15, 16, 26, 28,
    33, 40
Columbus, Christopher, 21
commercial banks, 31
copper, 8, 12, 15, 17
corrosion, 16
Cortés, Hernán, 6
cotton fiber paper, 32
counterfeiting, 14, 30, 32, 35
counting machines, 15
country money, 31
cowries, 6, 8
credit, 30, 38
credit cards, 38, 39
cuneiform writing, 12
currency exchange, 40, 41
Cyrus, king of Persia, 34

Dark Ages, 13
debit cards, 39
denominations, 14, 31, 34, 36
design, 32, 34
Diners Club, 39
dollar standard, 41
dollars, 6, 7, 10, 29, 31, 40
Domesday Book, 13
double entry system, 13
drachmas, 9, 12
drying, 15
ducats, 10
ductility, 18
duPont, John E., 35

edges, 14
Edward I, king of England, 6
Eight Reale pieces, 20
El Dorado, 19
electronic banking, 6
electrum, 9
Eliasberg, Louis, 17
elixirs, 29
engravers, 32
Este family, 17
European Union, 40

euros, 6, 40, 41
exchange rates, 41

Fargo, James, 41
farthings, 6
Federal Reserve banks, 7, 15, 28, 31
field, 14
finance agreements, 38
florins, 10
flying money, 30
fool's gold, 23
forgeries, 14, 30, 32, 33, 35, 40
Fort Knox, 28

Garrett, T. Harrison, 17
gold, 6, 7, 8, 9, 10, 14, 16, 17, 18-20,
    21, 22-23, 24, 25, 26, 28-29, 41
gold bullion, 28, 29
Gold Coast, 18, 22
gold dust, 29
Gold Rush, 23
gold standard, 29, 41
goldsmith's notes, 7, 31, 36
grain, 9, 12
Great Depression, 6
Great Roll of the Exchequer, 13
greenbacks, 31
grid squares, 17
groats, 6

halfpennies, 6
heads, 14
Henry VII, king of England, 10
Herpin, Georges, 35
Hill, Rowland, 34
hire purchase loans, 38
Hong Kong Heritage Museum, 37
HSBC bank, 37

identity theft, 39
Inca, 13, 20
income tax, 7
ingots, 6, 28
inscriptions, 14
inspections, 15
installment payments, 38
intaglio plates, 32
International Monetary Fund (IMF), 6, 28
Inverted Jenny stamp, 35
iron disulfide, 23

Joachimsthalers, 7, 10
John Jay Pittman collection, 17

Khan, Kublai, 30
korunas, 40

legends, 14
letterpress printing, 32
libres, 12
Louis Eliasberg collection, 17

Marshall, James W., 22
Mastercard, 39
Mayas, 6
Medici family, 17
Meegeren, Han van, 33
Mestrelle, Eloye, 14
metal detectors, 17, 26
Michelangelo, 33
Middle Ages, 22, 28, 34
milled coins, 14
mining, 18, 21, 22-23, 24, 25, 29
mint marks, 14
mints, 7, 9, 14, 15, 20, 28, 40
money orders, 36
Mongols, 30
Morgan, Henry, 21
museums, 17

nails, 8, 9
New York Chemical Bank, 38
nickel, 17
nitric acid, 23, 29
Noss, Doc, 26
Noss, Ova, 26

obols, 9
obverse side, 14
offset lithography, 32
Oresme, Nicole, 6

Pacioli, Fra Luca, 13
panning, 23
paper money, 6, 7, 10, 29, 30, 31, 40
papyrus, 13
pennies, 7, 10
Penny Black stamp, 34
Personal Identification Numbers (PINs), 38, 39
pesos, 41
philately (stamp collecting), 35
phishing, 39
pictograms, 8
pictographs, 12
pieces of eight, 20
Pipe Roll, 13
pirates, 20, 21, 26

Pitt, William, 7
Pizarro, Francisco, 20
planchets, 15
platinum, 28
Polo, Marco, 6, 30
post offices, 34
postal system, 34
potassium carbonate, 22
potlatches, 8
pounds, 10
prospecting, 23

quipus, 13

rands, 40
Rand mines, 18
Red Book Guide to U.S. Coins, 17
reliefs, 14
reverse side, 14
rim, 14, 15
Royal Canadian Mint, 40
Royal Exchange, 7
Royal Mints, 14, 40
rubbings, 16
Russia Company, 7

screw presses, 14
scribes, 12
security, 32
sequins, 10
Seward, Edward, 21
Shetland Isles, 26
shipwrecks, 26
shoppers' plates, 39
silk notes, 30
silver, 7, 8, 9, 14, 16, 17, 20, 21, 26, 28
Simjian, Luther George, 38
Singapore dollar, 40
smart cards, 39
sonar detectors, 26
Spanish Main, 21
stamp collecting, 35
stamp hinges, 35
stamp tongs, 35
stamps, 18, 34-35
Stevenson, Robert Louis, 27
stock market, 7
storage vaults, 15
store cards, 38, 39
storing, 16
striking, 15
substitute checks, 37
sunken treasure, 26
Swiss francs, 40

swords, 7, 8

T. Harrison Garrett collection, 17
tails, 14
tally sticks, 13
tax records, 26
taxes, 7, 13
Teach, Edward, 21
thalers, 7, 10
themes, 16
tobacco, 7, 31
tobacco notes, 31
tokens, 12
tool coins, 8, 10
tools, 8
touchstones, 14, 29
trade, 6, 29
trade potlatches, 8
traveler's checks, 41
treasure, 19, 20, 21, 26-27
Treasure Island (Robert Louis Stevenson), 27
Treskilling yellow stamp, 35
Trial of the Pyx, 6, 14

U.S. Mint, 7, 15
U.S. Treasury, 31
unsecured credit, 39
upsetting, 15

Vinci, Leonardo da, 15
VISA cards, 39

wampum, 7
washing, 15
watermarks, 32, 33
webbing, 15
weight, 9, 12, 14, 25, 28
Wendela (ship), 26
Wetzel, Don, 38
William the Conqueror, 13
Wimmer, Jenny, 22
Wimmer, Peter, 22
Wong Cheuk Hin, 37
writing, 12, 13

yen, 10
yuan, 10, 41

zinc, 15